Adagio Days

Amelia Fielden

Adagio Days

it doesn't feel
as if time is flying, or
standing still –
one adagio day
follows another now

Adagio Days
ISBN 978 1 76109 568 9
Copyright © text Amelia Fielden 2023
Cover photograph by 'pling, Terns, Bulli Beach, 2016
Azure exhibition and launch, 2017
with thanks to Fabian Prideaux and Kathleen Bleakley

First published 2023 by
GINNINDERRA PRESS
PO Box 3461 Port Adelaide 5015
www.ginninderrapress.com.au

Contents

Preface	11
Foreword	13

Individual Tanka

Tanka Strings & Sequences

Cries Louder Than the Surf	33
Always Something	34
'Whatever the bird is, is perfect in the bird…'	35
Family Members	36
Wing Beats	37
Moments	38
Some Stones Too Heavy	39
The Sound of Waves	40
When Will This Ever End?	42
A Woman's Scent	43
True Love Stories	44
Plus ça Change	45
Some Days I Hardly Converse	46
Night Garden	48
Still Swimming	49
Umbrella Alerts	50
Gong Thong	52
From the Sixth Storey: 24 Hours	53
Yuki	56
Pink Hyacinths	59
Words Words Words	62

Tanka Stories

Till We Meet Again	65
Always Roses	66

'Pretty Bubbles in the Air'	67
Grooves of Change	69
Acceptance	70
Talking the Walk	74
The Elephant in the Room	75
That Old Chestnut	77
Hanabi	78
New York New York	81
Raked Gravel	82
A Tale of Two Cakes	83
The Swan Downunder	86
White Crane	87
And In Ukraine	88
Praying Hands	90
Four Quartets	91
Grandson	93
'Round Up the Usual Suspects'	96
Plans Cancelled	97
Not the Pony Express	98
The Violin Sobs	100
Once Upon a Time	101
Shiny Black Shoes	102
Singalongs	103
A Taste for Brandy Alexanders	105
Here, There, and Everywhere	106
Jags of Light	108
Finding Pearls	112
Yuko's Fans	114
red orange yellow green blue indigo violet	116
Decisions	117
'Time is everything and nothing at all'	118
Lime Milkshakes	119

Eau de Nil	121
Life in the Sky	122

Responsive Tanka Pieces

Not Again	129
Conversations in Tanka	130
Seven Colours Blending	133
A Crowd of Memories	135
Flowing Colours	137
Many Shades	139
Tanka Chain 'Colour'	140
Awash in a Dream	141
Waxing and Waning	143
Still Hanging On	145
Our Wise Years	147
A Face in Every Window	149
Moving Closer	151
A Tanka Rainbow	153
Wisteria Branches	155
In the Blink of an Eye	158
Fireflowers	160
Daytrip – a rengay	162
About the Author	163

This book is dedicated to my daughter
Kathleen Miriam Bleakley
my inspiration, mentor
and loving companion in Wollongong

Preface

The word 'adagio' is Italian for 'slowly', from *ad agio*, 'at ease', and it is most often used to designate a leisurely tempo in music.

Almost all of the poetry in this collection has been written since mid 2021, when I moved permanently, with my elderly groodle Yuki, from a house in Canberra to a retirement village apartment in Wollongong.

The move has brought me much closer to my dear daughter and fellow writer, Kathleen – to whom this book is dedicated – and back to the Tasman Sea coast that I have always loved.

Barely a fortnight after my new life had begun, Wollongong was placed into lockdown. The vast open views from my sixth-floor apartment, of both the ocean to the east and the escarpment to the west, became even more important to me than I had imagined.

Although the situation here is more relaxed now, I still lead my life in a leisurely manner.

Early mornings, there's a busy twittering, singing, squawking from all sorts of birds as they start their day.

Late at night, I hear the sighing of the surf and thumping of the waves on Coniston Beach in the middle distance, and frogs kero-kero-ing in the garden ponds.

In between, are my adagio days.

Amelia Fielden

Foreword

O lucky reader, there is much to enjoy here.

The adagio is often where composers inscribe their most memorable and heartfelt music played at a slow or leisurely tempo: think Beethoven's Moonlight Sonata or Samuel Barber's Adagio for Strings (made famous in the film *Platoon*). While this collection is certainly memorable and heartfelt, I should warn you there's nothing leisurely here.

These are four pleasures ahead of us.

First is the variety in tanka poetry. Amelia has been writing and editing tanka for many years (this is her ninth book of original poetry in English) and she is an expert or sensei of the form. Here we see tanka as a single verse; as a string of verses elaborating on a theme; tanka as part of an associated narrative; and as responsive writing collaborating with poets in Canada, the USA and Japan, as well as Australian poets, each voice distinct and chorusing off the other.

A second pleasure is the range of subject matter. As many of these pieces were written while Australia and the world faced restrictions due to Covid-19, themes of separation and isolation feature as do reconnections made through FaceTime and Zoom. There is the abrupt end to a friendship as in 'Lime Milkshakes', family and childhood memories such as 'The Elephant in the Room', as well as longer meditations such as the passing of a beloved mentor in 'Yuko's Fans' or the decline of Yuki, the poet's cherished dog. There are also joyful humorous pieces: a grandson's first concert, a first flight in a jet plane, a mother's role reversal as a solicitous daughter brings groceries and checks that the poet is eating properly, and the discovery of a different kind of multitasking as the poet composes tanka during leisurely laps of the pool ('Pink Hyacinths').

And I should mention the songs – everything from *Rigoletto*, and *The Pearl Fishers*, to Irving Berlin and Judy Garland adds musicality to many of the poems.

A third pleasure is the intimacy of the writing. Many of these pieces have been published elsewhere but brought together they provide a multifaceted picture of the poet at 80. Here she is in her sixth-floor eyrie watching golfers, dog-walkers and surfers, communing with the local birdlife and continuing to write.

Our fourth pleasure is imagination. Tanka is distinguished by plain language and a broad range of subject matter. For me, this makes it interesting poetry that speaks to the joys and disappointments of a life lived every day. In its five lines it also allows space for the reader to join in the creative effort, to enter an imaginative or dreaming room. Take for example this award-winning piece:

> stroking slowly
> through cool blue silkiness
> I lose concern
> for things I can't control –
> the sun will set at seven

Consider the spaces between the sensuality of swimming, the loosening of daily worries and the sunset – both aphoristic as some hard-won wisdom and suggesting that the swimming (and life) will continue into the evening regardless of effort. Like the pauses in Moonlight Sonata, it's in the spaces between the notes where our imagination takes flight.

What lucky readers we are to have such a rich collection of poetry to engage with and enjoy.

Peter Frankis
Convenor, Poets in the City and Poetry Appreciation Groups
South Coast Writers Centre
January 2023

Individual Tanka

Published in *The British Haiku Society Anthology in Memory of Linda Jeanette Ward*

music vibrates
from his Slovakian flute
the blue
of mountains far away
beyond my climbing

Published in *Cattails* (online) Journal

Beethoven's Ninth
my father listening in tears
taught me
the joy of a symphony
and that men cry too

Published in *Eucalypt*

slow morning
rain slides down the panes
in silence
the ghost of a small dog
nuzzles my dangling hand

early Wednesday
white on aquamarine
waves breaking…
an eagerness of surfers
launches into the foam

this morning
like some sentimental song
a rainbow
and the sweet tweets of birds –
Omicron waves roll on

stroking slowly*
through cool blue silkiness
I lose concern
for things I can't control –
the sun will set at seven

* This tanka received a Scribbly Gum award.

Published in *Leaves: a tanka anthology of nature*

a little skink
slithers across my path
into long grass –
keeping a low profile
with Omicron rampant

seagulls flapping
in a fresh-water pool
apparently
rinsing salt from their wings ---
all the things I'm still learning

Honourable Mention in the Mt Fuji Tanka Grand Prize Contest 2021

my granddaughter
stands atop Diamond Head,
I'm on Mt Keira –
texting is the only way
we can cross the ocean now

Published in the anthology *Poetry for Ukraine*,
edited by Robin Barratt

        destroyed
        by Russian bombardment
        a hospital
        for women, children, babes –
        my useless fury of tears

Published in *red lights*, responses to Saito Mokichi tanka

Saito Mokichi

    this sky
    beyond the eastern mountains
    steeped red
    in the red
    morning-glow

Amelia

    the sun sets
    behind the escarpment
    blazing
    through my western window
    with the day's last flames

Saito Mokichi

    how bright
    the sun's orb
    turning turning
    and these very pussy willows
    beginning to glow

Amelia

    moving around
    my sky-high apartment
    the sun rises
    red from the eastern sea,
    sets gold in the western hills

Published in *Ribbons*, Journal of the Tanka Society of America

sleeping in death
all of my lovers, now
I wake daily
in this body imprinted
with long ago caresses

Ribbons Tanka Hangout music theme

Mother's Day
by great-grandma's clifftop grave
her six daughters
harmonising Galway Bay –
the Pacific sighs below

Published in *Ribbons* Tanka Studio

goodbye theme

> holding him
> in the palm of my thoughts
> holding him
> in my arms no longer –
> third anniversary

response to photo
of a footprint in sand

> dear cousin
> always ahead of me,
> is that you
> out beyond the surf break –
> I paddle through the shallows

response to photo
of no trespassers sign
in the snow

> borderless love –
> flying from summer heat
> across the world
> to a White Christmas
> for family, always family

Published in *Self Portraits*, Tanka Society of America anthology 2022

        in full thrum
        cicadas emphasizing
        the summer days –
        less is more, I tell
        my tanka students

Published in *Song Birds*, 2022 anthology of the United Haiku and Tanka Society

      happy waking
      to calls from waterfowl
      and the pling pling
      of an incoming text
      from someone who loves me

      the straight lines
      of two white egrets
      arrowing
      across a sky-blue sky –
      quo vadis, quo vadis

not a tanka; written for a meeting of the Tram Stop Poets

I Walk Around Spring

inhaling fragrance
from gardenia bushes;
noticing new leaves
on frangipani branches;
counting cream flowers
in old magnolia trees;
admiring purple
agapanthus in bloom;
tracing with my eyes
red kangaroo paw curves;
smiling at the smiles
of yellow-petalled daisies;
listening to a magpie
arguing with itself

and a 'found' tanka from the above

inhaling fragrance
from gardenia bushes,
noticing new leaves
and counting cream flowers
on old magnolia trees

and one haiku, published in the anthology of the Haikudownunder conference

spring deluge
huddled under the eaves
damp kookaburra

Tanka Strings & Sequences

Cries Louder Than the Surf

learning to swim
in a beachside pool
filled, frothing
with salty coolness
from the Tasman Sea

same blue sea…
two golden dogs racing
down the sand
splashing through the shallows
surfing gentle waves

same blue sea…
a bearded swimmer bouncing
our granddaughter
over spraying breakers
calling come in, come in

same blue sea…
new families playing
in and out
the swirling sucking tide
seaweed streamers lift and shift

same blue sea
on a long horizon…
white gulls drift
above my balcony
cries louder that the surf

published in *International Tanka*, Japan

Always Something

that rising sun
a bright yellow blob
wobbling
over the ocean rim –
is our earth really round

flying past,
a pelican squadron
commences
Sunday's ceremonies –
coffee comes to the boil

across fairways
the first golf carts trundle,
dawn clouds disperse –
Nothin' but blue skies
from now on…*

breaking the peace
a rescue helicopter
heads for the beach –
always something to see
from my sixth-floor balcony

why do surfers
carrying their boards
run down the sand –
those waves keep rolling
rolling rolling rolling

* Irving Berlin's 'Blue Skies'
published in *International Tanka*, Japan

'Whatever the bird is, is perfect in the bird…'*

dancing
through the zen garden
in silence
a pair of honeyeaters –
I meditate on feathers

paddling smoothly
among water lily drifts
a pelican
highlights the landscape –
if only I could paint

a cormorant
sharing the wash of wild waves
in the sea pool
bobs up, floats on weedy froth
…dives down, away from me

white corellas
flocked on the power lines
swaying, swaying
in ferocious winds –
how long can we all cling on

a blue heron
plumaged in grey and white –
how I loved
the variety of colours
in pencils I used as a child

* Judith Wright, Australian poet
published in *International Tanka*, Japan

Family Members

French windows
mostly kept closed now…
on the inside
smudged nose prints left
by our last labrador

once more I dream
of leading my pony
to his paddock,
escorted by three pet dogs –
long gone now, all of them

grey afternoon
raindrops drip dripping
down the panes…
the ghost of a golden dog
begs a familiar lap

the vet asks
whether I want fifty, or
a hundred
heart pills for my white pooch
hopeful, I take the hundred

suddenly
the wind's in her whiskers
and she's frisking
like the puppy she was
too many years ago

published in *Kokako*, New Zealand

Wing Beats

every morning
after a languid night of love
we stroll around
the shores of a shallow lake
that shimmers beyond our inn

no need to hide
from swans and water hens
roaming wild
in rural seclusion
on this obscure island

the last day
before separating
we linger
near a small egret
bright white in misted reeds

months later
you send me a framed photo
of flying swans –
I write you a short poem
about our final egret

published in *Kokako*, New Zealand

Moments

a tradie sits
outside the vet surgery
cradling
his limp border collie…
socially distanced

researching
a lost old friend on google,
I'm directed
to her online funeral –
why did I wait so long

two bouquets
of red roses delivered
at once –
is husband doubly sorry
for missing my birthday

carrying
his clarinet, grandson
mounts the stage –
will he recall the notes,
I'm holding my breath

unexpected call
from my doctor's office
'please come in
as soon as possible' –
after a routine breast screen

published in *Kokako*, New Zealand

Some Stones Too Heavy

swimming
my first and lasting
liberation
Dad's patient coaching
in Coogee's ocean pool

playing
netball, tennis, squash
never strongly
somehow keeping up…
lively school and uni years

the joys
of cradling babies
carrying kids
in moves round the world
such a rich life

these arms
paralysed by polio
in '45,
rehabilitated
now support me in old age

published in *Milestones* anthology, Australia

The Sound of Waves

this sunrise
too spectacular for words…
another day
with my dog and poetry
another month of lockdown

six seagulls
floating on rose-gold clouds
in the dawn pool –
no painters or poets here,
just golf buggies passing

swifts dancing
above the sand dunes,
surfers boarding
the deep sapphire swells –
life seems normal for some

pink and grey
galah-plummage sky,
dreaming beach…
once a day is enough
for all the bad news

three ships anchored
along the horizon
storm clouds massing
more wartime restrictions
Delta still winning

bangalow palms
squawking with cockatoos
at twilight
a pond dulling to pewter –
when will we meet again

published in *red lights*, USA

When Will This Ever End?

clouds bisect
an uncertainty of sky,
tiresome
entering a third year
of mask-wearing caution

gazing outside
from my zoom position
I envy
the wide-wheeling seagulls –
under the desk, a white pooch

Yuki dog
lies close to the computer,
her soft snores
rising with the readings –
I mute my audio

standing still
on their black reflections
at the pool's edge
two red-beaked moorhens
free to choose when to fly

unscented night…
the wind howls round my dream
of spring rains
in Tokyo, stripping
petals from cherry blossoms

published in *red lights*, USA

A Woman's Scent

her perfume
Evening in Paris
and my mother,
nowhere to be found now
except in fond memory

lavishly splashed
with 4711
cologne, Grandma
waiting for Grandpop
to come home from work

stashed away
at the back of a drawer
his last gift
of musky scent – I don't want
my body to smell like that

Je Reviens
'I will come again'…
if only
I could return to Paris
wearing this loved fragrance

embraced
by my surfer granddaughter,
I inhale
the salt scent of the ocean
from her bronzed shoulders

published in *red lights*, USA

True Love Stories

an old lover
half a century later –
oh, dear Alex
in my heart you were
always so much taller

my little girls
saved up and bought a lovebird*
for Great-grandma
'to keep her company'
when she lost Great-grandpa

a cousin's husband
disappears into dementia –
she tells me,
tending him dutifully,
'I love the man he used to be'

weekly bridging
wishes and reality,
I Facetime
my far off grandchildren…
this electronic love

celebrating
sixty years of a love match,
they order
from the restaurant menu
very different dishes

* in Australia 'lovebird' is a colloquial term for budgerigar
published in *red lights*, USA

Plus ça Change

sometimes silver
sometimes aquamarine
sometimes sapphire
viewed from my balcony
sea colouring this lockdown

masked again
spectacles fogging up
I peer
at the supermarket shelves –
what do my pooch and I need

beyond touch
not yet beyond reach
family voices,
dear faces, sharing screens
in twenty twenty-one

young woman
with a kelpie running
on wet sand –
so many dogs, and beaches,
loved in this long lifetime

a liner glides
across the horizon,
white on blue
herons flap into the sky
I am here, missing you there

published in *Ribbons*, USA

Some Days I Hardly Converse

unknown birds
chirping from shrubbery,
gulls fluttering
in the memorial pool
rose-gold sunrise reflections

a grey heron
skipping here and there
over the grass
rises into graceful flight
as golfers swing closer

silly galahs
strolling across asphalt
chittering
as if wondering
where they parked the car

visible
in the azure sky
a duck-shaped cloud
and one like a crane
feathered wings spread wide

ornamented
with rainbow lorikeets
low railings
on my sixth-floor balcony –
where is the camera

blown sideways
by a southerly buster,
white bird-rags
litter the tumbling sky…
what else might change now

published in *Ribbons*, USA

Night Garden

a last walk out
before our bedtime
the dog's leash
looped smooth over my fingers
paving stones slick underfoot

outlined in lights
anchored cargo vessels
dividing
ocean darkness and
the sky's black velvet

from the distance
that rhythmic roar and suck
of the sea,
in path-side ponds frogs drone
their mating rituals

around the grounds
no night-scented stock flowering,
but nuanced smells
from close-planted shrubs
spice the humid air

a beach child once,
all senses sated again
at the coast
am I imagining
the taste of salt on my lips

published in *The Crow*, Australia

Still Swimming

paralysed
by polio, her arms
are moved gently
back and forth, round and round
in a hospital pool

day by day
week by week, month by month
persevering
with therapy, until
finally some feeling

Dad delights
in teaching her to swim…
buoyed by salt,
chuckling at seagulls
she plays in the beach pool

water becomes
the beloved element
soothing her way
through the years and places
of a long, rich, life

hydrotherapy
will be your friend, counsels
her knee surgeon –
I know, oh I know
says the octogenarian

published in *The Haiku Way to Healing* edited by Robert Epstein

Umbrella Alerts: excerpts from a 2022 La Niña tanka diary

February 9
dismal Monday
this coastal La Niña
hovering
even the seagulls
complain of the rain

February 11
blurred ship-shapes
glide along the pencil line
between dim sky
and gunmetal ocean –
where is summer hiding

February 24
a flotilla
of pelicans sailing
the golf course,
sodden lorikeets
huddling on my balcony

March 5 watched
through salted windows, the sea
heaves grey and white
while I hunker down
in a blue armchair

March 9 my little dog
walks diagonally
ears flapping
in the howling wind
drenched streets start to dry

April 8 a rain bomb
explodes over the 'gong,
I google
instructions on how to
construct an ark

published in *34–37 Degrees South*, South Coast Writers' Centre digital anthology 2022

Gong Thong*

mysterious
like the singles you find
on beaches
there's just one – this one
is not rubber or plastic

glazed porcelain
blue on a white foot-shape
this 'gong thong'
reimagined from a thong
abandoned on City Beach

a surfie
carrying board and towel
runs to the sea
on the heel…mid-sole
a mini steelworks smoking

beneath the toes
underwater creatures
wriggle and writhe
in the lively willow pattern
of another culture

* response to Gong Thong by Gerry Wedd, 2007, Ways to Water exhibition, Wollongong Art Gallery, 2021
published in South Coast Writers' Centre anthology 2022

From the Sixth Storey: 24 Hours

roiling surf
under thunderous skies
celebrating
this dramatic finale
to my placid day

waking early
with a bright rainbow arching
through the dullness
might I go flying, like
those happy little bluebirds*

torrential rain
has flooded the golf links…
players absent
ponds are populated
by homecoming gulls

white hyphens
punctuate the wild sea
where a sail
struggles with the wind
to stay vertical

---

* in the song 'Somewhere Over the Rainbow' from *The Wizard of Oz*

treetops sway
as clouds climb over the scarp
a heron lands
on my balcony rail –
no need for conversation

this morning
the heron stays still
long enough
for me to take its picture –
next, a rainbow lorikeet

rain rain rain…
the golf course is a lake,
cranky parrots
shelter at the French windows –
at least I can't be flooded

'On Wings of Song'
Mendelssohn's creation
flies from my room
to a passing pelican…
sultry afternoon

singing along
with Charles Trenet on YouTube
'La Mer'
in another hemisphere
and in my study window

pastel cloud-drifts
closing a warm day
background music
from the dusky ocean
a silver-winged rise of gulls

the sky displays
a golden moon-ball
then wraps it
in the night's navy velvet
frog sounds grow louder

Yuki

first hard lesson
learned as a child, the lifespan
of a pet dog –
our time together too short,
ten loved, nine lost

deep in dark night
listening to blinds creak
and Yuki snore,
I wonder how many more
mornings we will have

on this grey day
the white dog wags with joy
when my daughter
appears in her green sweater
and orange alpaca scarf

this morning
the sea is sullen,
not so
my elderly dog
prancing along the path

sunny day –
ever the optimist
I purchase
a comfy new bed
for the 'ancient pup'

back to the vet :
we agree Yuki should have
one more chance
surgery on her tumour
scheduled for next week

can't concentrate
my dear old Yuki
not eating
and miserable –
how long should I wait

nothing sadder
than a sick pet who
can't say
what is wrong, where it hurts –
the vet takes blood samples

'wait and see' day:
nothing good to see,
waiting now
for the vet to call
to make a decision

a calmer time,
the sky has cleared again
my hopes
not high, but rising –
more spring flowers each day

have I found
the right rhythm to comfort
and ease these days
as she drifts lovingly
towards a final sleep

Pink Hyacinths – snapshots of my new life in a retirement village

       a cloud shaped
       like the flying kangaroo
       up and away
       all those years of travel…
       rereading old diaries

       white cockatoo
       paused on a blue fence
       wings tucked in
       choosing to stay there,
       free to roam the skies

       renewing
       my passport for five years,
       renewing
       my dreams of foreign parts –
       for now I stroll the gardens

       a water hen
       standing on her reflection
       at the edge
       of the Memorial Pool –
       how will I be remembered

       my daughter
       brings me green vegetables
       and fresh fruit,
       checks I'm eating properly –
       this role reversal

legs feel like new
since my massage visit,
only problem,
the rest of me so old –
time for a 'nana nap'

pink hyacinths
growing in china bowls
perfume her room…
neither of us stoops now
to conquer garden beds

a thunderstorm
takes out our power …
sixth-floor dwelling
without an elevator
such a long walk down

gourmet evening :
a Valentine's dinner
shared
with other residents
who have lost their loves

Links cinema   'Shall We Dance' –
long before Richard Gere,
hand in hand
with a high-school boyfriend
watching *The King and I*

Links Cinema   Robert Redford
so like my teenage crush…
all oldies now
yet *Out of Africa*
feels ageless to me

morning pool,
swimming so slowly
I can compose
tanka in my head –
multitasking at eighty

French practice
with another ex-teacher,
all the while
'The Last Time I Saw Paris'
resonating…

brain gym:
weekly quiz in the village
eager seniors
pushing pulling lifting
mental equipment

doves murmuring
gulls skimming the surf line
swifts air-dancing…
one more balcony day
communing with the birds

Words Words Words

the prof writes
on the board, Japanese
has three scripts –
what a challenge, I'm hooked
for the next sixty years

old teachers
at our high school reunion…
sports' mistress
turns her back, spurning me,
head of French kisses my cheeks

I focus
on studying Spanish
to help grandkids –
they drop the subject, then
covid closes down tripping

at eighty
I discover new words
for Scrabble
in the dictionary
and a zeal to win

learning to zoom
zooming to learn, my mind
expands
as my movements contract –
maybe I'll travel next year

published in *International Tanka*, Japan

Tanka Stories

Till We Meet Again

a lone surfer
riding grey-green waves
this long morning
I wait on the beach
for the clouds to roll by

Pandemic weather hangs over fortress Australia as normal life stalls. Once more there are separations from loved ones. Part of every war, such separations.

four ships anchored
along the horizon
storm clouds mass
more restrictions
Delta still winning

During World War I, believed at the time to be 'the war to end all wars', an American popular song* included the lines 'When the clouds roll by, I'll come to you / Then the skies will seem more blue'.

day's end sky
faded blue, streaked pink and gold
wraps this city
quietened by Covid lockdown…
what colour might hope be

* 'Till We Meet Again', 1918; lyrics by Raymond B. Egan, music by Richard A. Whiting
published in *Adversity*, an anthology edited by Robin Barratt

Always Roses

Home from the office, I'm contemplating my courtyard garden when the call comes from my daughter: 'Tia dog was in too much pain, so…'

> *summer's end*
> *golden roses blooming*
> *in the blue dusk*
> *how can she be lifeless*
> *while we still love her*

Twenty years on from that sad evening, the lover who gave me those bushes is farewelled in a live-streamed covid funeral.

> *bright fragrance*
> *unfading memories –*
> *how we touched*
> *through every year from youth*
> *to withering old age*

I deadhead the roses, then sweep the courtyard again…

published in *A Toast to Poetry*, collected work by the Majura Café Poets, 2020

'Pretty Bubbles in the Air'*

One summer Sunday we set out for the short drive to Karkeek on the western edge of suburban Seattle. Packed to the max with children, Border Collie, picnic gear, frisbee, bats and balls.

High on a cliff above Puget Sound, this park has everything for a family day in the outdoors: vast swaths of grass, a playground, hiking trails. Down the steep iron staircase, and parallel to train tracks, a strip of pebbly beach scattered with rock pools.

And today, the Bubble Man. On the tray of his ute parked beside the central lawns, is balanced a big tub of soapy water. Dipping his hooped wand into this tub, he magics streamers of giant, iridescent bubbles.

> *an old man blows*
> *his fragile creations*
> *into the blue*
> *seagulls 'fly so high,*
> *nearly reach the sky'*

Kids come running from every direction. They leap and squeal, trying to catch the uncatchable.

The bubbles burst, as bubbles always do.

> *dog passed away*
> *children no longer children.*
> *I exist now*
> *in a single's bubble*
> *on the far side of the world*

* from the first verse of the 1918 song composed by John Kellette and others

> *'I'm forever blowing bubbles*
> *Pretty bubbles in the air,*
> *They fly so high, nearly reach the sky,*
> *Then like my dreams they fade and die'*

published in *cattails*, online journal

Grooves of Change*

'Ti Amo'
half a century ago
pulsing
from the turntable
in tune with my love affair

I'm chatting with my young – well, thirty something – hairdresser about his new apartment. He tells me he's having some extra cupboards made. And that the carpenter was mightily impressed by the collection to be housed in them.

'Records? You mean vinyl?' I ask.

'Yeah.'

I natter on about the 33s with which I had reluctantly parted in my second-last move.

'Actually, mine are all 45s. I've collected about 2,000 of them.'

expect
the unexpected
so often said,
but really…single plays
in twenty twenty-two?

---

* 'Let the great world spin forever
down the ringing grooves of change':
Alfred Lord Tennyson's poem 'Locksley Hall'
published in *cattails*, online journal

Acceptance

a collaboration between Amelia Fielden (A) and Jan Foster (J)

this quiet night
as a sad year departs
I'll replace
longing with acceptance –
my agapanthus stand tall

In December 2019, embraced by the love of family visiting from USA, I still feel young, irrespective of my birth date.

2020 has turned me into an old person. Plans for adventures at home and abroad sabotaged by Covid-19. I am isolated from my grandchildren and many of those who animate my life.

No fireworks this New Year's Eve. But tomorrow I'll plant the Golden Bunny rose bush a friend has given me to mark my birthday.

A

small birds dart
in and out of shadows
restless
with the season's turning
life beginning to stir

Forced by circumstances to spend the festive season alone at home, I wander out to sit in my garden. Honey-eaters flit and flutter among the branches of a large bottlebrush, sipping nectar and chatting to each other. Watching them, something deep inside me sparks back to sudden life, why not create my own virtual garden, a gathering of photographs of all my missing loved ones – friends and family alike – where I can sip and sup whenever I feel lonely. I reach for my phone to order a large corkboard online, so I can start to plan my garden of faces, to feed my soul. J

perched on the fence
sulphur-crested cockatoos…
I send photos
to a distant granddaughter,
'my favourite birds', she texts back

Their father posts pictures on Facebook of the teenaged siblings standing in the snow, ready to hike up the mountain behind. I see that my grandson is now a bit taller that his older sister.

The next day, during our Facetime chat, I comment on this to Stephen.

Yep,' he confirms, 'and my New Year resolution is to catch up to Dad.'

I may be shrinking, but they are still growing, and that's wonderful. A

clear as a wish
in the rising light
a feather
drifting on the air
floats away out of sight J

In the sugared almond colours of dawn, I am standing on the shore of Australia's surf coast, lost for words. Later today, I'm to deliver the eulogy to my sister, lost to us through melanoma. We had always loved the beach as children, so I thought spending some time here might spark inspiration for a fitting tribute to her. In the soft hiss of retreating waves around my bare foot, I seem to hear her voice:

'Don't go all maudlin on me. Tell them of the fun we had. Recount the silly things I did, especially the ones that shocked everyone. I'll be there. You don't think I'd miss out on this bit, did you?'

In the fading echo of her laughter, a gull launches over the water into the morning sun.   J

published in *CHO, Contemporary Haibun Online*

Talking the Walk

strolling through
my village grounds
out the security gate
onto a short street
turn left, left again
another short street
hearing the waves
up the golf course slope
smelling of salt
        there it is
        the ocean
always the same
always different

private pleasures
to regulate and pass
lockdown days
greeting other dog walkers
checking out the surf

published in *CHO, Contemporary Haibun Online*

The Elephant in the Room

every Wednesday
dinner at Kensington
with roast beef
rice pudding, Tiny the dog
and very best manners

When finally allowed to leave the table, accompanied by Tiny her pet Pomeranian, I would explore great-aunt Sophia's seldom used Edwardian drawing room.

A treasure cave: paintings with gilt frames, china figurines in glass-fronted cabinets, a piano draped with gold and silver fringed shawls, a jardinière of peacock feathers…

Below a cupid-clasped mirror, the ormolu mantelpiece. There, amid a clutter of crystal vases and enamel boxes, knelt an elephant. An ornate porcelain elephant wearing a headdress studded in gems, and on its back a howdah ready to transport a rajah and his entourage.

Standing on an embroided footstool, I would reach up to touch it. Aware of my fascination, the lady of the house promised this elephant would be mine when I was grown up.

Sophia, our wealthy relative without direct descendants, was in the habit of making and remaking her will, with detailed directives for the distribution of her many possessions.

Which is why my family did not believe Alec, her much younger second husband when, after Sophia's death, he swore there was no will be found.

In the absence of a will, Sophia's entire estate, including diamond jewellery earlier allocated to my grandmother, an annuity for my grandfather, Edward, and my precious elephant, automatically became her husband Alec's property.

Almost immediately Alec sold the house and disappeared. Never to be seen again in Sydney.

no forty thieves
just an evil Ali Baba
acting alone
ransacked a treasure trove
and broke the family bonds

Until I was fifty, I believed what I had always been told: that Sophia was my great-aunt, my maternal grandfather's much older sister. Then, a researching cousin discovered she was in fact our great-grandmother, who at sixteen had born a boy, Edward, out of wedlock; 'father unknown' inscribed on his birth certificate.

family stories
genteel lady living
a family lie
my beloved elephant too…
how few survive

published in *CHO, Contemporary Haibun Online*

That Old Chestnut

A poet friend brings some roasted chestnuts to our group. Her daughter is now selling them on Fridays at the Canberra market.
Instantly I am back.

> *in Paris*
> *as winter sharpens*
> *my dark lover*
> *buying bags of chestnuts*
> *from a street seller*   1985

> *in Nara*
> *as golden leaves fall*
> *my fair lover*
> *ordering chestnut parfaits*
> *at an ice cream parlour*   2004

> *the texture*
> *of those distant seasons,*
> *those affairs*
> *saturating my senses*
> *as I peel a chestnut*   2021

I share the bag of chestnuts, not my recollections

published in an issue of *CHO, Contemporary Haibun Online*, as its featured piece of tanka prose

Hanabi*

My lifelong fascination with fireworks began when I was about six. At the time, my grandfather was working for the navy. One summer evening, we boarded a naval launch, motored out towards Sydney Harbour Bridge, and moored on the dark water.

The sky became black velvet, sequined with stars. Suddenly the stars were pink and green and gold: booming   flashing vanishing.

> *the boat rocks*
> *as I scamper side to side*
> *looking upwards*
> *for the most beautiful*
> *of the flower fire**

In my childhood, 'Empire Day' was a special event on the May calendar. Families celebrated by letting off crackers in their gardens at night.

circa 1949
> *in safety*
> *behind the kitchen window*
> *I waved and yelled*
> *at Dad outside, firing off*
> *catherine wheels, fountains, rockets*

Fireworks, a time-honoured tradition in Japan. In rural villages particularly popular is the custom of playing with sparklers on summer nights. Kids run around excitedly weaving light patterns into the darkness.

Yamaguchi	*my small girls*
prefecture	*clad like the locals*
August 1976	*in yukata†*
	as they dance down the street
	waving magic wands

---

* The Japanese term for fireworks is *hanabi*, which literally means 'flower fire'.
† Yukata are cotton kimono, worn informally especially in summer.

Many years ago, all of those hanabi, all of that fun.

And then, the end of 2021. After two pandemic years of separation, our widely-scattered family was finally, if briefly, re-united.

New Year's Eve   *ten together*
2021   *waiting on my balcony…*
                         with a huge bang
                         the sky explodes in rubies
                         emeralds, silver, and gold

A joyful gathering as ephemeral as the fireworks.

2 January   *through salty air*
2021   *crickets shrilling on one note,*
                         a rolling roar
                         from the blacked-out ocean…
                         no flower fire, this lonely night

published in *CHO, Contemporary Haibun Online*

New York New York*

…not a dream I ever-dreamed, yet now this award, this chance. The gift of flights and three nights in a hotel on Manhattan.

At 4 a.m., the grinding and clanking of garbage trucks starts my one free day. Later, after strawberry waffles in the breakfast café, I make my own way to the object of today's aspiration – the Metropolitan Art Museum.

'You need a whole day for it' is the received wisdom and a whole day it is, from the Egyptian halls to the Tiffany stained glass, to the Impressionist gallery.

At closing time, I stroll back through Central Park in spring. Dogwood trees in frothy blossom. Scarlet tourist carriages trotting past.

I come to a strange artificial cliff. On a huge flat rock at its tip there's a wedding ceremony happening.

The bride's long blonde hair flows beneath her veil. She places her hands into those of her African-American groom.

Fragrance drifts from beds of daffodils and jonquils lining paths to the exit.

> *more foreign*
> *for me, than Tokyo,*
> *this city*
> *so familiar from song*
> *New York, New York*

---

* a response to the lyrics of 'Empire State of Mind', by singer-songwriter Alicia Keys

published in *CHO, Contemporary Haibun Online*

Raked Gravel

no other word
but 'dancing' could describe
the progress
through the Zen garden
of a black butterfly

So much of what I love about Japan is here, in the grounds of this old wooden temple. One hundred metres, and several hundred years, up the cobbled lane from a major thoroughfare, such peace.

at noon, empty
of priests and worshippers
this temple precinct
thrums with a transience
of summer cicadas

My guide today is my dearest Japanese friend, Nariko.
There is a deep understanding, and almost half a century, in our relationship.

How fortunate I am to sit with her now, sipping green tea under the veranda eaves, as we silently contemplate that dancing butterfly…

published in the *Cultural Identity* anthology edited by Robin Barratt
previously published in *Mint Tea From a Copper Pot & other tanka tales*, Amelia Fielden, 2013

A Tale of Two Cakes

Once upon a time, when I was a poor student in Tokyo, I happened to meet at the railway station another poor student, who lived in the same humble lodgings. Strolling home together we came to a stop before the window of a glamorous patisserie.

'Oh, look,' exclaimed Mariko, 'mont-blanc…of course, it's autumn now.'

As an Australian raised on lamingtons and fruit cake, I had no idea what she was talking about. With a hungry gleam in her beautiful brown eyes, Mariko explained that mont-blanc is a type of cupcake, topped with pale brown chestnut puree in the shape of a mountain, and crowned with a whole candied chestnut.

Japanese food is very seasonal, and chestnuts are an autumn specialty.

We added up our yen and bought just one small mont-blanc between us.

Back in Mariko's diminutive tatami-matted room, we shared the cake and a pot of green tea. Delicious!

Two years later, diagnosed with tuberculosis, Mariko left the piano academy and went home to Kyushu to die.

> *sometimes I dream*
> *of that other life, and*
> *of Mariko*
> *forever twenty-three*
> *all these years I have lived*

Another era, another part of Japan. No longer poor, I was dining in late spring with a charming university professor.

On the dessert menu I found 'ajisai mont-blanc', hydrangea mont-blanc'. Curious, I asked for this when my companion ordered coffee. With a bow the waiter presented, on a plate decorated with real, purple, hydrangea petals, a classically-formed mont-blanc cake, whose chestnut puree was coloured the same purple as the flower petals.

Of course… May is the season for celebrating hydrangea in Japan.

indulging me
with the exotic cake
I fancied,
he smilingly denies
my stronger desires

he and I
so much in common
so much to say
both loving this country
alas not each other

In the summer of the following year, enjoying an afternoon snack of perennial red bean buns in Kyoto with a poet colleague, I recounted to her my mont-blanc episodes.

'Ah,' she commented, 'through those two cakes you have truly experienced *aware*, the pitifully transient nature of life and love.'

> *my life*
> *is what it is, still*
> *contemplating*
> *Japanese tanka*
> *love, longing, and loss*

published in the *Cultural Identity* anthology edited by Robin Barratt
previously published in *Mint Tea From a Copper Pot & other tanka tales*, Amelia Fielden, 2013

The Swan Downunder

Katy and I are learning ballet. Her mother tells the story of being taken, as a child, to see Anna Pavlova perform in Melbourne. A program including the great Russian ballerina's signature solo, 'The Dying Swan', with music by Saint-Saëns. Many years later, I find a black and white film of this on Youtube.

her arms flutter
she quivers en pointe
pas de boureé
to and fro across the stage,
Le Cygne…

slowly slowly
down on one knee, she sinks
folding into death –
a feather from her headdress
drifts through the spotlight

published in *Drifting Sands*, online

White Crane

The all-stops night train cuts through the northern snow country, tunnel after tunnel. Crammed with people returning home from Tokyo for the New Year holidays. A uniformed attendant comes along selling little earthenware pots of green tea, capped with handleless cups. My friendly neighbour, a young man in a shiny blue suit, offers me a mandarin from a red net. We introduce ourselves. It is 1963 and he is curious about my foreign presence. Where am I from? What am I doing here? I'm a research student from Australia, I explain. He compliments me on my Japanese. The second son of a rice-farming family, he is working now in a city electronics factory. I smile and nod to compensate for my difficulty understanding his rural dialect. It's late, the heating is stuffy, I'm sleepy. I lean my head against the window…

The train jars to a halt. An official voice announces arrival at the terminus.

Opening my eyes, I find an empty seat next to me. On my tray I discover an origami crane, traditional symbol of long life, folded from a paper napkin.

> *one lifetime*
> *so many meetings*
> *too many*
> *farewells…travelling*
> *landscapes and mindscapes*

published in *Drifting Sands*, online

And In Ukraine

We were wartime babies, Canberra High School's class of '58. Sixty-three years on, survivors who live in this area are still in touch. Some are close friends, others more like casual contacts.

In the second half of the second year of the pandemic, we began turning eighty.

By November, the Covid situation seemed to be sufficiently under control for an optimistic plan to be made: we would hold a macro joint birthday celebration in the New Year. Then along came Omicron…

> *anxiety*
> *contagious as Covid*
> *comes worrying*
> *through the calls and emails*
> *from elderly friends*

> *they are saying*
> *we are vulnerable*
> *they are saying*
> *masks are mandatory, and*
> *there will be another war*

numbers taken
restaurant reserved
menu chosen…
stoic yet cautious
we decide to postpone

unspoken
fear that 'normality'
may not return
in our ebbing lifetimes –
families and gardens grow still

published in *Drifting Sands*, online

Praying Hands*

brushing back
my damp straggly hair,
soothing fevers,
grandmother's cool hands
soft, so soft...

A sickly child, often confined to my room in those days when prolonged bed rest was believed to be a cure-all. Hour upon hour, while my mother washed and cleaned and cooked for the household, her mother would sit by my bed.

No television, no iPads back then – just patient love.

Gran would read aloud story after story from books Dad found in second-hand stores. In between, she would sing: 'You are my sunshine, my only sunshine', and old Irish ballads. All the while her long-fingered hands smoothing pieces of foil from chocolate wrappers, making them into silver balls on the little table at her knees. When the balls were almost the size of my hands, I'd sit up and we'd play rolling them back and forth. The silver balls and her broad gold wedding band glinting and gleaming across the table. Then lying back, I'd hold out my hand and, with Gran's fingers lightly touching mine, drift into sleep.

I never saw my grandmother's hands clasped in prayer.

* written in response to the engraving *Praying Hands* by Albert Dürer (1471–1528)
published in *Drifting Sands*, online, in its 'Repairing and Healing' issue

Four Quartets

A while ago I watched, on the big screen at my senior's village, the DVD of an all-time favourite movie, Quartet. Set in a home for retired musicians, its plot revolves around four former opera stars and their rendering of the iconic *Rigoletto* quartet – *Bella figlia dell'amore*, Beautiful daughter of love – in a fund-raising concert there.

Afterwards, I sat with memories of the full opera, and its delights, at different stages of my life.

'Now,' whispers my father, leaning into me. We're seated in the narrow gallery at the back of Canberra's only theatre in the 1950s. I am seventeen, and it's the first time for me to see an entire opera performed live – Giuseppe Verdi's *Rigoletto*.

This is the last act, and we have come to the quartet sung by the Duke of Mantua, Maddalena, Rigoletto and Gilda. I've listened to the record at home many times, and know the opera's story. But now…

> *a small stage*
> *a touring second cast*
> *and I*
> *don't understand Italian –*
> *bewitchment, pure and simple*

McCaw Hall, Seattle, 2018. *Rigoletto* set in a sinister Trumpian America. Another onstage quartet. *Bella figlia dell'amore.* Spellbinding again, always.

corruption
in contemporary costume
the four singers
voices soaring, weaving
through the music of Verdi

Recently, another viewing of this nineteenth-century masterpiece. Not in a theatre, but in the local cinema. Showing there is a film of the New York Metropolitan Opera performing *Rigoletto*. This time set in the Weimar Republic. Best quartet I've heard. Finally, a heart-stopping suspension of disbelief.

Gilda, stabbed
dying, lies on the stage
singing
farewell to her father,
Rigoletto, ah…

published in *Drifting Sands*, online

Grandson

i) Still Perfect

a special voice
calls from across the sea
'come soon,
the blossoms are starting
Grandma, come soon'

So I fly from Sydney to Seattle, arriving late at night in the wake of a windstorm. Next morning as we walk to school, up the hill street under deep pink double-petalled cherry blossoms, Stephen mourns, 'They were much better yesterday, before the storm.'

Then he picks up a fallen flower and hands it to me. 'This one's still perfect, though.'

precious moments
as the years speed by
dearest boy
when I'm not here, always
remember I loved you

ii) Op.15 No.1* Seattle, 5 August 2016

A summer morning. sunlit green maple leaves crowd into the tall opened windows.

Between them, an upright piano. Wearing only superhero underpants and orange socks a child is playing Schumann.

'Scenes from Childhood'
overlapping joy
in this boy
in this music – unearned,
the richness of my life

* 'Scenes from Childhood', composed by Robert Schumann

iii) True Measures

His outfit is new: white shirt, black tie and trousers, shiny lace-up shoes. But the focused face as he walks onto the stage, holding his clarinet, is not new to me. I have seen that expression many times – when he mounts a starting block at the pool, when he crosses a finishing line at the track, when he sits down at the piano…

a long while yet
until he becomes a man –
the conductor
raises her baton,
this is the beginning

published in the *Family* anthology edited by Robin Barratt

'Round Up the Usual Suspects'*

Pre-Christmas lunch gathering 2020. The end of a calamitous pandemic year. None of us infected by Covid-19. But there have been losses: two husbands, a son, a grandson. Cancers. Surgeries. Exacerbation of chronic illnesses.

Yet thirteen from the class of '58 have made it here. All in still manageable health and in positive spirits.

On the veranda of a village restaurant we toast the safe arrival of a first great-granddaughter.

> *old roses climb*
> *clinging to the trellises…*
> *round our table*
> *schoolgirl voices tell stories*
> *of their generations*

* an iconic utterance in the film *Casablanca*, which was released in 1942, the birth year of most of my schoolmates.
published in the *Friends and Friendship* anthology edited by Robin Barratt; previously published in the Majura Poets' Chapbook, 2021

Plans Cancelled

not quite dawn
the first birds chirping
and closer by
my dog softly snoring…
what shall we do today

In 2020 I became an old person. Until then, my determination, sense of adventure, and love for family and friends scattered around the globe, had kept me feeling young, irrespective of my birth year.

A pandemic obliterated the longed-for trip to visit my grandchildren in Seattle, and eroded my confidence in travelling.

late spring
light in my courtyard
suffused
with golden roses…
'sheltering in place'

published in *International Tanka*, Japan

Not the Pony Express

The postman was a very important person, when I was a child.

Six days a week he tramped our suburban streets, a huge leather satchel slung over his shoulder.

Each time he put something into the front fence letter box, the postman blew his whistle.

> *birthday greetings*
> *invitations, letters*
> *bills for Dad*
> *Christmas cards once a year…*
> *the thrill of his whistle*

In preparation for my year at university in Nagoya, Gran purchased a stock of fifty blue aerogrammes. Every week, she wrote me the family gossip and her love. Postie – Gran never knew his name, though they shared twenty years in Coogee – would sound two blasts on his whistle whenever he had a letter with Japanese stamps.

highlights of news
from 'the country upstairs'*
recorded
in Gran's exercise book –
waves echoing on the shores

Older than Gran was then, I listen on Tuedays and Thursdays for the motorbike delivery of my mail. Even now, a personal touch. A young man born in Laos comes into the courtyard to greet my dog.

'Yuki, my friend'…
not yet quite paperless
this new world,
kookaburras chortling
from the garden wall

* *The Country Upstairs* is a travelogue on Japan, by Colin Simpson.
published in *International Tanka*, Japan

The Violin Sobs

Walking down the hill from home to Coogee beach, with Dad.

Then along the prom to our Saturday night treat: the triple bill at the Coogee Boomerang cinema. Brighter than the lights from the lamp posts flashed its neon frontage.

From that last time…why was it the last time, I wonder… the movie I remember is *Limelight*. Probably not really appropriate for a twelve-year-old.

The story of an ageing clown and a suicidal young dancer.

Unforgettable, its heartstring-plucking theme song that soared, as a down-and-out Charlie Chaplin lay dying in the wings of the theatre while his beloved ballerina, Claire Bloom, spun across the stage.

> *how black and white*
> *'I'll be loving you,*
> *eternally'* –*
> *the myriad shades*
> *of my life and loves*

* 'I'll be loving you, eternally' is the theme song from *Limelight*.
published in *International Tanka*, Japan

Once Upon a Time

Springtime in Tokyo. Cherry blossoms froth over paths around cages at Tama Zoo. Entranced by monkey families, my small daughters keep asking to go back to their antics. Then they want to see the elephants. It's not a large zoo. Two elephants confined on a rectangle of concrete. One swinging its trunk listlessly. The other just stands there, gazing out into the distance beyond high iron fences. Next, a solitary tiger. Pacing back and forth, back and forth, back and forth, on a narrow walkway outside an artificial cave. Giraffes and zebras share a patch of scruffy grass. Somewhere, a lion roaring. Enough. The children are easily diverted with ice creams and more monkeys.

At the exit there's a souvenir shop – of course. I'll buy them a soft toy to share. They choose a small brown monkey. 'What will we call him?' 'Hanky pants,' I suggest, improvising a nappy for him from my checked handkerchief as we train into the city.

Back home, the girls gather together their toy animals, introduce Hanky Pants, and all play tea parties.

> *generations*
> *of visits to a zoo*
> *generations*
> *of children's tea parties –*
> *how fortunate I've been*

published in *International Tanka*, Japan

Shiny Black Shoes

February 1952

The man from Legacy stands tall on the primary school stage.

Flanking him are ten-year-old girls in their ordinary cotton frocks, heads hung down, eyes on their shiny black shoes.

The man from Legacy explains to the assembly that, thanks to the generosity of his organisation, he is here to present Susan and Helen with cheques to pay for their school uniforms, books, and stationery supplies this year.

Because they have no fathers, only mothers.

Because they are wards of Legacy.

On the headmaster's signal, teachers encourage applause.

Legacy kids
fathers lost in the war
dignity
lost in their school hall –
Lest We Forget

published in *Kokako*, New Zealand

Singalongs

Mother's Day
by great-grandma's clifftop grave
her six daughters
harmonising Galway Bay –
the Pacific sighs below

Lots of songs, lots of singing, in my childhood. Gran crooned lullabies to the littlies, hummed and sang as she went about her chores.

In my house, always music from the radio and from records Dad collected.

I never learned to play an instrument. But I could pedal a mean pianola. There were several pianolas among our extended families. And in the flat of great-aunt Clara stood a baby grand. That was the centerpiece of numerous clan gatherings.

Every occasion called for a party. Every party called for Clara's son-in-law, Keith. He would play by ear anything from 'How Much is That Doggie in the Window' to the Moonlight Sonata, ragtime to waltz time. Not a lot of room for dancing, but some couldn't resist 'The Blue Danube'. Requests were Keith's forte: if you could hum the first bars of a piece, he could play it. Lyrics no problem either; prodigious recall, my relatives.

Beer and soft drinks, sausage rolls and cream sponges. Mostly it was about the singalongs.

> *a warm wind*
> *ruffles songs of yesteryear*
> *through my hair –*
> *I still remember the words*
> *and how you all sang them*

published in *Kokako*, New Zealand

A Taste for Brandy Alexanders

college days
one of the few students
always on time
for meals, tutorials
new experiences

Phillip was an older man. Much older. The uni boys were just… boys.

Outside of lectures they revolved around kegs of beer and easy girls.

She didn't want to be an easy girl. To become a nuanced woman she needed a summer affaire.

Phillip had a profession, an apartment, a cream Volkswagen. He was subtly instructive. Over their months together he encouraged her to sample everything on the sweets' trolley in fine-dining hotels.

autumn winds
blew them off course
over the ocean
more to learn
in another life

published in *Ribbons*, USA

Here, There, and Everywhere

Soon after I started in 4th grade, my father's office transferred us from a comfortable urban existence with extended family in the metropolis of Sydney, to Canberra. In the early 1950s our capital city felt like an under-resourced country town.

To compensate all of us, I was sent back to Sydney to stay with my grandparents five or six times a year. So began 'here and there' for me.

> *escaping*
> *up up and away*
> *with TAA**
> *to my preferred home,*
> *calling cousins the next day*

At twenty-one I was given, not 'the key to the door' – I already had that – but a passport and a scholarship to study in Japan.

Off into a new world, 'the country upstairs'.† Ever since, I've had two lives: an Australian life and a Japanese life.

> *an outsider*
> *in a foreign culture*
> *delighting*
> *over the differences…*
> *gum leaves   cherry blossoms*

---

* TAA was once a domestic airline in Australia.

† *The Country Upstairs* by Colin Simpson is the author's impressions of Japan and its people following World War II. It was my Sydney lover's farewell gift to me.

While this duality continued, another 'there' stepped onto my retirement stage. My elder daughter moved to Seattle. I was blessed with American-born grandchildren.

A love triangle, Australia, Japan, USA, here, there, and everywhere.

> *always planning*
> *my next visit over there*
> *the only way*
> *I could bear to leave*
> *one passion for another*

And then, anywhere but a narrow 'here' was made impossible by a pandemic.

> *grey drapes of cloud*
> *closing this warm day*
> *background music*
> *from the dusky ocean*
> *a silver-winged rise of gulls*
>
> *bangalow palms*
> *squawking with cockatoos*
> *at twilight*
> *a pond dulling to pewter…*
> *when will we meet again*

published in *Ribbons*, USA

Jags of Light

A collaboration between Marilyn Humbert (M) and Amelia Fielden (A)

> *cloudless night*
> *starlight and moonbeams*
> *everything*
> *edged with silver…*
> *I hear wild things singing*
>
> M

Tonight the grandkids are visiting for sleepover. Time to light the backyard campfire. Cook potatoes wrapped in foil, damper twists on eucalypt sticks, and toast marshmallows. Everyone takes turn to choose songs for the singalongs. While the fire dies down, there are bush tales of bunyips, and cattle droving. Mostly we sit quietly together…watch and listen.

M

watching street lights
go on at dusk, off at dawn
through small windows...
in my city childhood
campfires lit only in books

A

Packing for her flight to a new life studying at the University of Hawaii, my granddaughter comes across a family photo from eight years ago, and texts it to me. There we all are at the beach on the Big Island. The kids in sunhats and swimmers kneeling by a wonky sandcastle. Blue-green sea smiling behind.

Ahead? Who knew, who cared, in that moment.

A

published in *Ribbons*, USA

jags of light
flash over waves…
I find calm
in the storm's eye
following my own path

You tell me again about the view we will see from the summit, a thread-like creek unravelling through the valley. I fall further behind as the bush trail continues upwards. I stop to catch my breath beneath towering blue gums. It's here I discover a patch of native orchids hiding in the understory of ferns, their tiny white petals bright stars among the surrounding green.

no signposts
at the intersection
I take a risk
on an unknown road
away from neon's dazzle

M

pandemic days
sitting outdoors not allowed…
though these paths
to my seascape are steep,
must keep on walking

'Keep on' is my manta for these strange and hazardous times in which we are trying to live. As restrictions cramp outside activities, the colours in nature seem to intensify: rose-gold clouds at dawn, green stretches on the golf links, cobalt ocean, scarlet grevillea blooms, the rainbow plumage of lorikeets… If only I could paint.

A

Finding Pearls

Just past our ninth birthdays, my cousin and I are sprawled on the lounge room floor, playing with his new Hornby train set.

Stopping his chuffing and tooting, Brian goes to the window and opens it wide. 'Listen.'

From the flat above, music.

Men singing: first one, then the other, then together.

The voices flood through me, though I can't understand their words.

Afterwards, 'What was that?"

'It's op'ra. In French. I like it.'

> *two singers*
> *harmonising, enchanting*
> *two children*
> *into a lifelong love*
> *for classical music*

Back home, I try to describe the 'op'ra'. Mum is preoccupied cooking dinner, but Dad pays attention: 'I think you're talking about the duet from an opera called *The Pearl Fishers*.'

Christmas comes. Under the tree for me, among several books, there's a record of Jussi Björling and Robert Merrill singing 'In the Depths of the Temple'. We play the duet three times that day.

Long lost to me now, that vinyl disc and the man who wept hearing it.

books and music
reading and listening
what greater gifts
from one generation
to another, than those

One afternoon sixty-five years later, I am in the Sydney Opera House. Excited by this first opportunity to see a full stage production of *The Pearl Fishers*. Act I, spell-binding.

At interval, the young couple seated in front of me stand, gathering up some parcels.

Leaning forward, I offer, 'If you like, I can mind those things for you.'

'It's OK, thanks. We're going now. We only came for the duet.

Well…

published in *Ribbons*, USA

Yuko's Fans

fluttering
her blue Kyoto fan
Yuko glances
round the respectful room,
sighs a sensei's sigh

The sensei* never raised her voice. Whatever challenges arose in the Tower Society's monthly tanka workshop were handled serenely, and with nuanced movements of her folding fan.

As a teacher of traditional Japanese poetry, Kawano Yuko most often wore kimono, with a seasonally accessorized fan tucked in the top of her obi. For her rare appearances in Western clothing, the fan was carried in a Gucci handbag, from which it was always the second thing extracted after her spectacles.

A closed fan was pointed at the person whom she wished to speak next. It was tapped on the table once to emphasise her point – or two or three times, indicating 'enough of that'.

And sometimes, regardless of the temperature in the classroom, sensei would waft an opened fan to and fro across her face.

I had been designated Yūko's official translator. In the Japanese autumn of 2009, we met to work together for the last time. My beloved mentor was already terminally ill. On parting, she presented me with one of her elegant fans. It has scarlet maple leaves painted on the palest green silk; too precious to use.

husky-voiced
fanning her flushed cheeks
the poet speaks –
my pen transforms her words
for English posterity

---

* *Sensei*, literally meaning 'before born', is the appellation given in Japan to one's superior, mentor, teacher, or an expert/specialist in any field from tea ceremony to medicine to motor mechanics.

published in *Ribbons*, USA

red orange yellow green blue indigo violet

The afternoon storm has passed. There's a well-defined rainbow arching high over the sea. Its radiance seems to flow from the foot of the northern lighthouse to the southern clifftop. More real, more vivid this rainbow, than any dream.

Yet for me it conjures a screen shot of pigtailed Judy Garland singing in that Kansas farmyard to her dog Toto, about 'happy little bluebirds' flying, as she longs to, to a land 'somewhere over the rainbow'.*

beyond this bay
far beyond its rainbow
lies a country
where I've flown for love
again and again

could wishing
upon a star, help me
to wake up
over there with my grandkids –
maybe a vaccine will work

* reference: 1939 movie *The Wizard of Oz*, and Dorothy's iconic song 'Over the Rainbow'
published in *Triveni Haikai*, online, India

Decisions

A toss-turn night. I wake on the floor beside my futon mattress. The scent of fresh-woven tatami mats sets me sneezing. Sliding open shoji screens reveals Hakata harbor at dawn framed in the tall windows.

a liner glides
past dark bonsai islands –
tomorrow
I'll take over this lease
and sign the divorce papers

published in *Triveni Haikai*, online, India

Time is everything and nothing at all'*

Nine years and one month since we adopted a 'senior dog', a little groodle (golden retriever x poodle) from a Canberra rescue society. We already had a pair of miniature labradoodles, Kin and Konni, whom we had raised from puppyhood. But my husband Arthur could not resist the groodle's charms. She was eight then, and called Lucy. We renamed her Yuki, the Japanese word for 'snow' as she was pure white.

Seven and a half years since we lost Konni to a brain tumour.

Five years and seven months since Arthur died, followed ten days later by golden boy, Kin.

Two and a half years since Yuki lost the sight in one eye.

Eighteen months since Yuki and I moved to The Links retirement village in Wollongong, and she began to lose the sight from the other eye.

Ten weeks since Yuki, now seventeen years old, was so ill that I thought the time had come…

> *breezes ruffle*
> *lily pads on the pond*
> *everyday*
> *my dog walks more slowly*
> *soon maybe not at all*
>   written on 24 November 2022

* lyrics from an original song, 'Eternity', composed by Australian musician Mikel Simic

Lime Milkshakes

Rituals of shared widowhood: Saturday afternoons watching DVDS on your big screen; Thursdays, Vietnamese takeaway dinners at my place, where you enjoy stroking the little white dog; movie matinees; sometimes lunch on the terrace of a café by the lake: grilled barramundi and salad with coffee for you, a lime milkshake for me.

Tough times, too: you looked after the little white dog when I flew to Melbourne to be with my daughter, and my son-in-law hospitalised with blood cancer, paralysed overnight. Only six weeks later, you drove me to his burial, three hours' away in Wollongong. Stayed with me all through that weekend.

The following year, when I tripped and ripped open my newly operated knee, you brought sandwiches to the Emergency Department, sat there with me for hours, then made us cuppas back at home.

I talked you through unsettling emails you showed me. Supported you in tricky situations with aged parents, and siblings. Shopped and cooked for you during an extended period of illness.

Last year, I moved from our city to live in Wollongong, close to my daughter. Several hours' drive between us instead of one suburb. Patterns of meeting were undone. But there would be visits back and forth. We'd still be in contact often?

Four months of covid lockdown. We messaged each other every few days.

Then a text: you'd decided to end our friendship. 'No point.' My protests and questions unanswered. Occasionally, in hours of sleeplessness, I think of those lime milkshakes.

> *morning sea*
> *waves rise break rise break,*
> *swallow dance*
> *past my balcony –*
> *what could I have done*

published in *Mantle*, the South Coast Writers' anthology, 2022

Eau de Nil

Silk scarf in lightish grey-green draped around a poet's neck.

Agatha Christie's *Death on the Nile*.

The fabled river flowing opaquely through Egyptian history.

That young woman, a stranger, at the university's spring ball on the arm of Hunter, universal heart-throb.

He called her Deidre.* A beauty with the whitest of complexions, and pre-Raphaelite auburn hair, who floated across the floor in eau de nil chiffon.

After his graduation, Hunter disappeared with Deidre into China.

Teaching English in Beijing, it was rumoured. Australia had no diplomatic relations with Communist China in those days.

Next I heard of them back in our country living in seclusion on a small farm. There – according to gossip – Hunter drank himself into an early grave.

(Christie's mystery was solved for me by Hercule Poirot. But I've wondered about Deidre.)

> *belle of the ball*
> *beloved of a maverick*
> *Deidre*
> *uncrowned queen of sorrows*
> *Deidre in eau de nil*

---

* Deidre is a name of Gaelic origin, meaning 'sorrowful'. In Irish mythology she is a queen known as 'Deidre of the Sorrows'.
published in *CHO, Contemporary Haibun Online*

Life in the Sky

pastel clouds
over the sunset ocean
silver gulls
dipping, swirling, turning
towards the shadowed shore

Yesterday, a heron arrowed through the air past my balcony. Almost close enough to touch, if I'd leaned over the railing.

a blue heron
plumaged in grey and white
how delightful
the colour gradations
of my Derwent pencils

I always love being up high, so it's no surprise that I've chosen to spend my eighties in a sixth-floor apartment in the coastal city of Wollongong.

Beethoven's Ninth
on the FM station,
white-capped waves
flecking the cobalt sea —
an armchair afternoon

This fascination with life in the sky began early. When I was nine, we moved to Canberra, away from Sydney and our extended family. For all the school holidays I was airmailed back to my grandparents – by TAA 'the friendly way', as the jingle ran.

> *innocent years*
> *led to my plane seat*
> *by Dad,*
> *met on the tarmac*
> *by Pop – no security*

Far from being scared flying solo, I was excited. Face pressed against window to scan the sights of miniaturized countryside and suburbs. Those amazing views from the air inspiring many a school 'composition' and poem.

> *DC3 rising*
> *above the toy town houses*
> *and matchbox trucks,*
> *lurching over Lake George,*
> *bumping down on the runway*

After graduating from university, I started travelling internationally. And continued to be a very frequent, enthusiastic flyer; until 2020 when the Covid pandemic clipped my wings and those of countless others.

My first experience of Qantas was to Japan in 1963, via refuelling stops in Manila and Hong Kong. Wonderful! Though disappointing to discover long-haul jets fly so high that the ground below is visible only for a while at take off and landing.

> *in my porthole*
> *drifting clouds pile on clouds –*
> *somewhere below*
> *the concrete skyscrapers*
> *of a metropolis*

At a lower level, my favourite fairground ride – alone or in company – is a ferris wheel. I've rocked in the sky many, many, times: by the water in Sydney's Luna Park, on reclaimed land in Osaka, over the harbour in Seattle, at Canberra's Floriade.

> *oh, ferris wheel**
> *go round, round, round*
> *memories last*
> *for you a single day*
> *for me a lifetime*
>
> by Kuriki Kyoko

It's over three years, now, since I was up on a ferris wheel, or in an aeroplane. These days I spend a lot of pleasurable time watching the ocean, and the flights of all kinds of birds.

> *riding the gale*
> *a screech of cockatoos*
> *wings past*
> *my apartment windows –*
> *another wild night ahead*

---

* my translation of the titular poem from *Ferris Wheel: 101 Modern and Contemporary Japanese Tanka*, which I co-authored in 2005

Responsive Tanka Pieces

Not Again

Amelia Fielden (A), Genie Nakano (California) (G), Kathabela Wilson (California) (K)

> *war in Europe*
> *Ukraines here lament*
> *and demonstrate*
> *on our TV screens –*
> *this feeling of helplessness*　　A

> *so brave*
> *women strapping weapons*
> *to their breasts –*
> *the cruelty of a dictator*
> *should not dictate*　　G

> *no borders*
> *at the world assembly*
> *hearts of nations*
> *beating together*
> *the drums of peace*　　K

published in *Colorado Boulevards Poets Salon*, USA

Conversations in Tanka

between Neal Whitman (California) and *Amelia Fielden*

first connections
new to tanka, I share one
with a friend
who suggests submission…
my first acceptance

editor's delight
getting a worthy tanka
from someone new –
wonder about our future,
'hope springs eternal'

collaboration
for us is conversation
without judgement –
suggested edits
offerings, nothing more

our seasons
opposite, time differences
tricky, we wield
pencils colouring in lives… *
now partners in poetry

* refers to *Colouring In: The Four Seasons of Four Poets*, Amelia Fielden, Gerry Jacobson, Genie Nakano, Neal Whitman, 2016

together we tour
my Point Pinos lighthouse –
her heritage
keepers of the Sydney light,
the span of friendship infinite

the years pass
with much talk of tanka,
books, movies –
our minds still meeting
across the Pacific

published by *Drifting Sand*, online

Seven Colours Blending

a responsive tanka rainbow written by Genie Nakano (G) and Amelia Fielden (A)

red sun above,
we stand barefooted
on mountain earth
anticipation
flowing through our blood   G

my small grandson
says his favourite colour
is **orange** –
having fun clothes shopping
for a new generation   A

long ago
a man in a **yellow** shirt
smiling gently
as sunshine poured down –
the scent of daffodils   G

blooming wild
over **green green** hillsides
around the lakes
one April when we were young,
ah, Wordsworth…   A

with a love
as deep as the ocean
we share lives
growing a new garden
blue morning glories   G

from farmed plant
to dye vat, to tablecloth,
this **indigo**
has come a long way
for our celebrations   A

a canopy
of pale **violet** wisteria…
meeting again
in springtime Tochigi
we walk through a fairy tale   G

is there something
somewhere over the rainbow* –
after the storm
seven colours blending
to lighten a grey sky   A

* reference to the song 'Somewhere over the Rainbow' sung by Judy Garland in the movie *The Wizard of Oz*

published in *Hedgerow* online journal

A Crowd of Memories

by Amelia Fielden (A) and Jan Foster (J)

    when freesias
    bloomed wild across the island
    I loved him
    long ago and far away…
    finding an old diary   A

    among the ruins
    of an old settler's cottage
    a sapling
    insisting on life
    for a new generation   J

    babies born
    in a pandemic
    locked out
    of their grandparents' arms,
    locked into history   A

after the storm
children emerging
celebrate
release into freedom
… rain-dancing in puddles   J

grey dawn clouds
drifting across the pink sky
overhead
a flight of five pelicans
journeys to the unknown   A

walking alone
along this deserted beach
I'm jostled
in a crowd of memories
from holidays passed   J

published in *Kokako*, New Zealand

Flowing Colours

by Amelia Fielden (A) and Jan Foster (J)

    this morning
    the sea stretches sky-blue
    to its edge
    a million waves
    from my grandchildren   A

    separated
    by a pandemic,
    the family
    texts birthday greetings
    …sharing my cake with birds   J

    on a small lake
    the single pelican
    preening itself
    perhaps for a mate…
    seated alone, I wait   A

an opal
in a setting of gold
flowing colours
as the new day dawns
a heron rises skywards   J

late night tryst,
one rose-gold earring
loosened , lost
found by her small daughter
on an Easter egg hunt   A

a slice of moon
a scattering of stars
this warm night
spread out before me
the feast of peace   J

published by *Kokako*, New Zealand

Many Shades

by Amelia Fielden (A) and Genie Nakano (G)

        in old age
        mirroring childhood
        my desires shrink
        to a room with a view
        of surf breaking on sand   A

        the footprints
        of a child, sand castles
        left behind
        I add some driftwood,
        my 'found art' creation   G

        those Sundays
        exploring galleries
        Dad and I
        no talent ourselves,
        just a love of paintings   A

        as we walk
        in the rose garden
        butterflies
        dancing to bird song
        …the sound of wings   G

        many shades
        of flowers, of pencils
        assembled
        for my return to colouring
        in a Covid book   A

published in *red lights*, USA

Tanka Chain 'Colour'

by Amelia Fielden (A) and Mari Konno (Japan) (M)

> your pink spring
> my golden autumn –
> seasons reversed
> yet parallel lives
> and shared memories   A

> the memory
> firstly, of a tanka fax
> delivered
> from Australia
> being all white   M

> white as snow
> my dog named Yuki –
> sadly
> she can no longer see
> out of her brown eyes   A

> eyes closed
> in the May garden
> sitting alone
> I am caressed
> by a soft green wind   M

published in *red lights*, USA

Awash in a Dream

by Amelia Fielden (A), Kathabela Wilson (K), Genie Nakano (G) Kris Kondo (KK), Susan Rogers (S), Dean Okamura (D) (members of Kathabela Wilson's USA Tanka Onsite group)

autumn beach	
deep blue sea, breaking white	
on golden sand	A
swan-shaped driftwood	
gathered for my birthday	K

ripples in the pond	
blur what is underneath	
glistening movements	G
as the Koi's greedy mouth	
swallows a cloud	KK

Strawberry Lake…	
dangling our hands	
over the boat's side	S
little waves caress palms	
clapping to the slow rhythm	D

steadily steered
with long poles, two punts
gliding the river   A
we pause for a picnic
among the water lilies   KK

far from home
afloat on the Doura River
I name clouds   K
drifting in the current
awash in a dream   D

published in *red lights*, USA

Waxing and Waning

by Amelia Fielden (A) and Marilyn Humbert (M)

        I sit
        remembering the past
        I sit
        contemplating the present –
        tide on the turn, already   A

        inkstone night
        howls of a dingo pack
        crisscross the plain
        waxing and waning
        the alchemy of moonlight   M

        urban child
        entranced by neon lights,
        now star-gazing
        by a billabong –
        which one to wish upon   A

Halley's comet
streaks east to west
I find comfort
in predicted events,
however remote   M

waking late
alone not alone
I'm greeted
by the familiar
happy dance of my poodle   A

in noon sunshine
we walk to the dog park
our escort
carolling magpies –
those bush-camping days   M

published in *Ribbons*, USA

Still Hanging On

by Amelia Fielden (A) and Marilyn Humbert (M)

    bridging
    wishes and reality,
    I facetime
    distant grandchildren
    smart phone passed back and forth   A

    sepia photos
    pasted three to a page
    in the album
    Dad wearing short pants –
    dust drifts through the attic   M

    overcast days
    leaves still hanging on
    as autumn starts
    we wait our turns
    for the magic vaccine   A

raucous noise
clouds of cockatoos
lift my mood…
the light and shade
of an uncertain future   M

over the park
a pandemonium
of parrots…
unperturbed, my old deaf dog
dawdles her way home   A

mass rally
chanting protesters
wave placards
'I am woman
hear me roar…'   M

published in *Ribbons*, USA

Our Wise Years

by Carole Harrison (C) and Amelia Fielden (A)

    you move nearby
    into a new home
    and lockdown –
    we zoom each other
    across the neighbourhood   C

    this dawn sky
    streaked with grey and gold
    a photo texted
    to my far off daughter –
    if only I could paint   A

    colours spread
    over a blank canvas
    smoothing
    the peaks and troughs
    of our wise years   C

in Japan
tanka are mostly sequenced
unevenly
to stimulate readers –
waves shaping in the sea   A

we once wrote songs
along distant shores
never ending
our cryptic sand-words
now savoured by the tide   C

published in *Ribbons*, USA

A Face in Every Window

by Gerry Jacobson (G), Mira Walker (M), Carmel Summers (CS), Rachel Colombo (R), Carole Harrison (C), Amelia Fielden (AF) and Ailsa Brown (A) (members of the Australian Lyrebird Tanka Circle)

quiet here now
I cook, she launders
we negotiate
what to watch
in the evenings　　　　　G

poetry night
a reader's voice
prevailing
past the zoom screen
the cat's tail　　　　　M

old tabby
sprawls on the sofa
soaking up sun –
for some, lockdown
is not a problem　　　　　CS

pet heaven
she is working from home
walks and hugs on tap
animal shelters
empty…for now   R

stoicism
learning to love living
alone … almost
the silence
between miaows   C

gazing outside
from this zoom position
I envy
the free-wheeling seagulls…
under my desk, a white dog   AF

online classes
writing, yoga, pilates
a screen and me –
stretching I walk outdoors
to sunshine, bush, bird song, sky   A

published in *Ribbons*, USA

Moving Closer

by Carmel Summers (CS), Mira Walker (M), Sue Donnelly (S),
Carole Harrison (C), Michelle Brock (B), Amelia Fielden (A)
(members of the Australian Lyrebird Tanka Circle)

        getting to know
        this new grandchild
        by video link
        longing for a real hug
        as well as smiles   CS

        pale peonies
        opening their flounces
        inside one
        the face of my grandma
        the softness of snow   M

        little child
        colour of honeycomb
        imagines
        a tribe of magpies
        chatting with the trees   S

years from now
will he remember kissing
an iphone screen,
trying to connect his finger
with my nose and ears C

intensive care
someone's much-loved mother…
just a gloved hand
and masked face
to ease a stranger's passing M

meeting 'for real'
after four months of lockdown
unmasked now
we move closer together
should we hug or kiss or… A

published in *Ribbons*, USA

A Tanka Rainbow

By Amelia Fielden (A), Sigrid Sarradun (S), Dean Okamura (D), Kathabela Wilson (K), Richard Matta (R), Jackie Chou (J), Genie Nakano (G), Susan Rogers (SR) (members of Tanka Onsite, USA)

soaked to the skin
during an afternoon stroll
rewarded
by a rainbow arching
over the flattened ocean   A

stunning spring
dew drops on the **red** petals…
quince blossom
radiant in contrast
to this morning fog   S

final farewells
orange tints through cloud drifts
rippling reflections
scattered on rolling waves
under the evening sky   D

as she was born
I named my daughter
Colleen,
seeing her as a little hill
covered with **yellow** flowers   K

wingbeats
of the **green** dragonfly
lifting my heart…
atop a lily pad a turtle
untucks its head   R

cloudless sky
his flute song deepening
in shades of **blue** –
how the world looks
without my coloured lens   J

my **indigo** child
born in a total eclipse
never cries,
her bright eyes shine
even on the darkest night   G

grandfather's ring
long lost in the Pacific
I see it now
in the mirror
of your **violet** eyes   SR

published in *Scarlet Dragonfly* online journal

Wisteria Branches

by Sigrid Saradunn (S) Amelia Fielden (A), Lynne Jambour (L), Genie Nakano (G), Kathabela Wilson (K), Kris Kondo (KK), Jackie Chou (J) (members of Tanka Onsite, USA)

century-old house
laced with wisteria
roof to ground
that was the year
they cut it all down   S

wisteria scars
marring the white façade –
who remembers now
those children playing with dolls
in the deep shade of the porch   A

in Florence
purple and white wisteria
cloaking
an ancient brick wall
behind the historic church   L

wisteria scent
flows through the home
forever
clinging to the walls
and long hallways   G

overgrown
and glorious wisteria
in old age
the mystery of loss
and disappearance		K

purple stains
on the wooden floors
wisteria petals
in the cracks –
will this house be haunted		G

near wisteria
the name acquired
from my ex-husband…
the children and I
hold onto it warmly		KK

swirling mist…
the wisteria blossoms
seem to float
above the geisha's head,
perfuming her skin		L

she ushers
wisteria into the house
still on the vine,
through a window
as if to save her life		K

bees are busy
in the wisteria blooms
a spring breeze
teases the wispy white hair
of an ancient gardener   A

golden cousins
to wisteria,
laburnum flowers
drooping down
over the fence   S

revisiting
my childhood home
drapes of wisteria
obscure the gate
I've long outgrown   J

wisteria petals
cover the walkway
to my father's house –
his lifelong warning
about my purple world view   J

over 33 years
a neighbour's cottage
on the hill
is swallowed up
by its wisteria   KK

published in *Scarlet Dragonfly* online journal

In the Blink of an Eye

by Amelia Fielden (A), Kris Kondo (KK), Genie Nakano (G), Kathabela Wilson (K), Dean Okamura (D), Sigrid Saradunn (S) (members of Tanka Onsite, USA)

New Year's Day
another chance to make
fresh memories –
an ocean pool swim
a lunch with cousins   A

new friends
zooming into my life
this year
always a balance between
undertows and ripples   G

flannel flowers
the comfort they give me,
their fuzzy charm
as I navigate one small
crisis after another   KK

shall we meet
in the Japanese garden
the tenuous 'yes'
of all in this pandemic…
the koi stare open-mouthed   K

under treetops
leaves sprout from twisted limbs…
light and shadow
aqua sky squeezes through
sparkles on the cold grass   D

uncertain times
savouring each experience
knowing life
can change its rules
in the blink of an eye   S

Fireflowers*

By Dean Okamura (D), Kathabela Wilson (K), Kris Kondo (KK), Amelia Fielden (A), Jackie Chou (J), Genie Nakano (G) (members of Tanka Onsite, USA)

morning chats
exploring the latest news
exploding like weeds   D
my childhood nightmare
dandelion fireworks   K

in sweeping arcs
kids write their names
with sparklers   KK
long summer evenings
in Japanese villages   A

dark day…
ready to burst forth
the fire within me   J
you're not listening
my temper on edge   G

the dragon lady
spitting sparks talons ablaze
above the rooftops J
breaking the tiles to bits
crashing into the parade D

with a great bang
the sky lights up in gold
silver and bronze A
mother shouts wonderful
her favourite blue multiflora K

the moment it happens
scarlet fireflowers
scatter G
and the heavens fill
with fading hearts KK

* in Japanese, *hanabi*

Daytrip – a rengay

by Amelia Fielden (A), Kathabela Wilson (KW), Kathy Kupka (KK), Sigrid Saradunn (S), Kris Kondo(K), Peter Larsen (P) (members of Tanka Onsite, USA)

storm passed,
a giant rainbow now
across the sea   A
can this be a bridge
to span our distance   KW

highway lanes
racing back and forth
over the river   KK
snapdragons on rails
daring humming birds   S

welcoming us home
freshly brewed coffee
in favourite mugs   K
two pairs of sandals
nestled by the door   P

About the Author

Amelia Fielden was born in Sydney, Australia in December 1941. She is an internationally awarded translator and poet.

Qualifications

Bachelor of Asian Studies (Japanese Honours) Australian National University, Canberra, Graduate Diploma of Teaching, Secondary Education, University of Adelaide, South Australia.

Graduate Diploma of Translation (Japanese) University of Canberra. Master of Arts (Japanese Literature) University of Newcastle, New South Wales; Masters' Thesis: An Annotated Translation of My Tanka Diary by Kawano Yūko

Career

1965–2003 researcher, teacher, translator.

Since retiring from full-time work as a senior translator of Japanese for the Australian government in Canberra, Amelia has specialised in translating Japanese literature – primarily, but not exclusively, tanka poetry.

Books Translated or Co-translated by Amelia

On Tsukuba Peak: 2000 tanka collection by Kawamura Hatsue; bilingual; Wollongong, NSW, Five Islands Press, 2002

Time Passes (Saigetsu): 1995 tanka collection by Kawano Yūko; bilingual; Canberra, ACT, Ginninderra Press 2002

Vital Forces (Tairyoku): 1998 tanka collection by Kawano Yūko; bilingual; co-translated with Yuhki Aya, Nagoya, Japan, Bookpark, 2004

Behind Summer (Natsu no Ushiro): 2003 tanka collection by Kuriki Kyōko; co-translated with Yuhki Aya; Canberra, ACT, Ginninderra Press, 2005

As Things Are: 100 tanka selected by Manaka Tomohisa from 10 collections by Kawano Yūko; Canberra, ACT, Ginninderra Press, 2005

On This Same Star ('Will'): 2003 tanka collection by Kitakubo Mariko; bilingual; Tokyo, Japan, Kadokawa Shoten, 2006

My Tanka Diary (Hizuke no Aru Uta): 2002 tanka poetry diary with prose commentaries by Kawano Yūko; Canberra, ACT, Ginninderra Press, 2006

Ferris Wheel: 101 Modern and Contemporary Japanese Tanka, the work of 56 Japanese poets; co-translated with Kozue Uzawa, bilingual; Boston, USA, Cheng & Tsui, 2006. Awarded the 2007 prize for translation of Japanese Literature by Columbia University, New York, USA; also known as the Donald Keene award.

Raffaello's Azure: tanka poetry and essays by Hazama Ruri; co-translated with the author; bilingual; Tokyo, Japan, Tanka Kenkyusha, 2006

Cicada Forest: anthology of the work of Kitakubo Mariko; bilingual; Tokyo, Japan; Kadokawa Shoten, 2008

Kaleidoscope: selected tanka of Terayama Shuji; co-translated with Uzawa Kozue; bilingual; Tokyo, Japan, Hokuseidō, 2008

Doorway to the Sky (Sora no Tobira): tanka collection by Tanaka Noriko; co-translated with Ogi Saeko; bilingual; Tokyo, Japan, Tanka Kenkyusha, 2008

Aster Flower (Shion): 2009 tanka collection by Kusumi Fusako; bilingual with colour plates; Tenri City, Japan, Tenrijihōsha, 2009

The Time of This World: 100 tanka selected by Ōshima Shiyō from 13 collections by Kawano Yūko; Baltimore, Maryland, USA, Modern English Tanka Press, 2010

Breast Clouds (Nyubōin): award-winning 2008 tanka collection by Tanaka Noriko; co-translated with Ogi Saeko; bilingual; Tokyo, Japan, Tanka Kenkyusha, 2010

Snow Crystal Star-shaped: anthology of tanka poetry by Konno Mari; bilingual, Tokyo, Japan, Kadokawa Shoten, 2010

The Maternal Line (Bōkei): 2008 tanka collection by Kawano Yūko; co-translated with Ogi Saeko; Baltimore, Maryland, USA, Modern English Tanka Press, 2011

A Bluish White Light 'a cry from the heart'; tanka about the Fukushima Nuclear Power Plant, by Satō Yūtei; edited by Yasunaga Tatsumi; Matsudo, Japan, JARC Corporation, 2013 (available on amazon.com in paperback or as Amazon 2014 Kindle edition)

Tanka to Eat: themed tanka masterpieces by modern and contemporary Japanese poets, selected and presented with commentaries by Tanaka Noriko; co-translated with Ogi Saeko; bilingual; Port Adelaide, South Australia, Ginninderra Press, 2014

From the Middle country (Naka no Kuni Yori); 2013 collection by Tanaka Noriko; co-translated with Ogi Saeko; Port Adelaide, South Australia, Ginninderra Press, 2015

The Journey of My Life: tanka composed by May Yen Ting translated by Amelia Fielden, with commentaries and prose translated by Steven Ting; edited by Ling-Erl Ting and Warren Wu; USA, Amazon Prime Paperback, 2014

Lovely Kimono: themed haiku and tanka by modern and contemporary Japanese poets, selected and presented with commentaries by Tanaka Noriko; co-translated with Ogi Saeko; Port Adelaide, South Australia, Ginninderra Press, 2016

For Instance, Sweetheart (Tatoeba Kimi); Forty Years of Love Songs; autobiographical essays and tanka poems written to each other by Kawano Yūko and her husband, Nagata Kazuhiro; first published in Japanese by Bungei Shunshu Tokyo, in 2011; Amelia Fielden, translated edition, Port Adelaide, South Australia, Ginninderra Press, 2017

Four Poets in a Boat: An Anthology of Contemporary Japanese Tanka; selected by Ogi Saeko; co-translated with Ogi Saeko; Port Adelaide, South Australia, Ginninderra Press, 2018

Poetry Bridges: Canberra/Nara Commemorative Anthology; edited and co-translated with Ogi Saeko and Tanaka Noriko; bilingual; Port Adelaide, South Australia, Ginninderra Press, 2018

Destiny (Unmei): a collection of Japanese tanka by May Yen Ting translated by Amelia Fielden; edited by Ling-Erl Ting and Warren Wu; bilingual; USA, Quadu Press, 2019

Two Countries (Kuni Futatsu): a collection of Japanese tanka by May Yen Ting translated by Amelia Fielden; edited by Ling-Erl Ting and Warren Wu; bilingual, USA, Guadu Press, 2019

Lily of the Valley: 2018/2019 tanka collection by Kusumi Fusako; bilingual with colour plates; Tenri City, Japan, Tenrijihosha, 2020

Original Poetry and Prose written in English by Amelia Fielden

Eucalypt and Iris Streams: poetry about Australia and Japan in various forms; bilingual, Japanese translations by Ogi Saeko; Canberra, ACT, Ginninderra Press 2001

Fountains Play and Time Passes: original tanka in English by Amelia Fielden, together with her translations of selections from Time Passes (Saigetsu) by Kawano Yūko; bilingual; Japanese translations of Amelia's tanka by Ogi Saeko; Canberra, ACT, Ginninderra Press, 2002

Short Songs: individual tanka poems and multi-tanka sequences; Canberra, ACT, Ginninderra Press, 2002

Still Swimming: individual tanka poems, plus multi-sequences and strings; Canberra, ACT, Ginninderra Press, 2005

Baubles, Bangles & Beads: Threaded Tanka; Canberra, ACT, Ginninderra Press, 2007

Light on Water: a collection of individual tanka, sequences and strings published between 2006 and 2010 in international journals and anthologies; Port Adelaide, South Australia, Ginninderra Press, 2010

Mint Tea From a Copper Pot & Other Tanka Tales: some stories of my life, in poetry and prose; Port Adelaide, South Australia, Ginninderra Press, 2013

These Purple Years: a collection of individual tanka, sequences and strings and tanka tales published between 2011 and 2017, in international journals and anthologies; Port Adelaide, South Australia, Ginninderra Press, 2018

More Farewells: a collection of tanka poetry and stories; Port Adelaide, South Australia, Ginninderra Press, 2021

Collaborations with other Poets

In Two Minds: response tanka in themed chapters, written with Australia poet, Kathy Kituai; Baltimore, Maryland, USA, Modern English Tanka Press, 2008

Weaver Birds: a bilingual responsive tanka diary written and translated with Japanese-Australian poet, Saeko Ogi; bilingual; Port Adelaide, South Australia, Ginninderra Press, 2010

Yesterday, Today and Tomorrow: a calendar year of responsive tanka written with Australian poet, Kathy Kituai; Brisbane, Queensland, Interactive Press, 2011

Words Flower From One to Another: responsive tanka in themed chapters written with Japanese-Australian poet Saeko Ogi; bilingual; Brisbane, Queensland, Interactive Press, 2011

Conversations in Tanka between Amelia Fielden, Jan Foster and Friends; several different forms of responsive tanka writing, composed by 23 poets from Australia, France, Japan, New Zealand, South Africa and USA; Port Adelaide, South Australia, Ginninderra Press, 2014

Colouring in: the Four Seasons of Four Poets: Amelia Fielden, Gerry Jacobson, Genie Nakano and Neal Whitman writing in Australian-American pairs, responsive tanka strings on spring, summer, autumn, and winter; Port Adelaide, South Australia, Ginninderra Press, 2016

Tanka Anthologies Edited or Co-Edited

Food For Thought: an anthology of new tanka on a theme, written by 45 Australians, collected and edited; Port Adelaide, South Australia, Ginninderra Press, 2011

The Melody Lingers On: an anthology of tanka on musical themes, written by 55 Australian poets, collected and edited; Port Adelaide, South Australia, Ginninderra Press, 2012

100 Tanka by 100 Poets of Australia and New Zealand – one person each; selected and edited by Amelia Fielden, Beverley George and Patricia Prime; Port Adelaide, South Australia, Ginninderra Press, 2013

Storyteller: individual tanka, tanka sequences (some written responsively with other poets) and tanka prose by Genie Nakano (USA), edited by Amelia Fielden and Ellen Weston; California, USA, Purple Aura Press, 2014

All You Need Is Love: the theme of 'love' interpreted broadly by 62 Australian poets; Port Adelaide, South Australia, Ginninderra Press, 2015

Poems to Wear: a Japan/Australian production; Part I; Japanese tanka selected, with added commentaries, by Noriko Tanaka, and translated by Amelia Fielden and Saeko Ogi; Part II Australian tanka collected and edited by Amelia Fielden; Port Adelaide, South Australia, Ginninderra Press, 2016

Poetry Bridges: Canberra/Nara Commemorative Anthology; collected, edited, and translated with Ogi Saeko and Tanaka Noriko; Bilingual; Port Adelaide, South Australia, Ginninderra Press, 2018

Leaves, tanka anthology of nature, edited by Amelia Fielden with the assistance of Liz Lanigan; Port Adelaide, South Australia, Ginninderra Press, 2022

(All of the above books published since 2013 by Ginninderra Press are still for purchase at www.ginninderrapress.com.au)

Poetry-related Activities

Member of the Japan Tanka Poets' Society since 1999

Member of the Tanka Society of America since 2000

Foundation Member of the Limestone Tanka Poets, Canberra, Australia

Member of the following Canberra poetry workshopping groups: Majura Poets, Moorings, The Poem Nest, Tram Stop Poets, Lyrebird

Tanka Circle; and the Wollongong groups Poets in the City, and Poetry Circles

English tanka and tanka tales published regularly in journals worldwide – for example in *Eucalypt* (Australia), *International Tanka* (Japan); *Kokako* (New Zealand); *Skylark* (UK), *Atlas Poetica, red lights, Ribbons* (USA); *Cattails, CHO, Haibun Today, Drifting Sands* (online); and in several international anthologies.

Presenter of translation seminars and tanka workshops in Australia, Canada, Japan, and USA

Participated in International Tanka Conventions in 2000 (Vancouver), 2006 (Honolulu), 2009 (Tokyo). In 2009 was one of the judges of the associated English tanka competition.

Appeared on NHK television programs with Kawano Yūko in 2000 and 2005.

Foreign guest representative at the Imperial Palace, Tokyo, for the Annual Imperial New Year Poetry Gathering, in January 2008

Other Interests

Travel, Japan, swimming, reading, writing, language studies; attending ballet and opera performances; enjoying the company of family, friends and pets.

www.ingramcontent.com/pod-product-compliance
Lightning Source LLC
Chambersburg PA
CBHW071454080526
44587CB00014B/2104